Hot and Cold

Terry Jennings

W
FRANKLIN WATTS
LONDON•SYDNEY

First published in 2009 by Franklin Watts

Franklin Watts
338 Euston Road, London NW1 3BH

Franklin Watts Australia
Level 17/207 Kent St, Sydney, NSW 2000

Copyright © Franklin Watts 2009

Created by Taglines Creative Ltd: Jean Coppendale and Honor Head
Written by: Terry Jennings
Design: Paul Manning

ISBN 978 0 7496 8725 0

Dewey classification: 536'.5

A CIP catalogue for this book is available from the British Library.

Picture credits
t=top b=bottom l=left m=middle r=right

3, 7, Gelpi, Shutterstock; 6, Peter G., Shutterstock; 8, 28bl, Digitalskillet, Shutterstock;
9, 28tl, Trutta55, Shutterstock; 10, 28br, Sonya Etchison, Shutterstock; 11, Fridamarija, Shutterstock;
12, Varina and Jay Patel, Shutterstock; 13, 28tr, Michael Macsuga, Shutterstock; 14, Robert Gubbins,
Shutterstock; 15, Charles F. McCarthy, Shutterstock; 16, 29tl, 29bm, Laurent Renault, Shutterstock;
17t, 29tm, Vince Clements, Shutterstock; 17b, 29bl, 29br, Sharon D., Shutterstock; 18, Jurgen Ziewe,
Shutterstock; 19, Matka Wariatka, Shutterstock; 20, Dmitry Melnikov, Shutterstock; 21, Popescu
Simona, Shutterstock; 22, Peter Baxter, Shutterstock; 23, Sasha Radosavljevich, Shutterstock;
24, Steffen Foerster Photography, Shutterstock; 25, Keith Levit, Shutterstock; 26, Mashe,
Shutterstock; 27, Peter Hansen, Shutterstock.

Franklin Watts is a divisi⟨...⟩ ⟨...⟩chette Livre UK company.

Contents

Hot and cold

Some things are hot. This kettle is hot.

steam

heat

STOP!
Never touch
a hot kettle or
put your hand
near steam.

▲ We know this kettle is hot because steam is coming from it.

Some things are cold. An ice lolly is cold.

▲ An ice lolly feels cold on your tongue.

The right clothes

Sometimes the weather is cold.
In cold weather we wear clothes
that keep us warm.

▲ These children are wearing thick clothes to keep them
warm in the ice and snow.

In summer, the weather is hot. In hot weather we wear cool clothes.

▲ This boy is wearing a hat, shorts and a t-shirt on the beach.

Food and drink

When the weather is hot, we like cold drinks and cool foods.

▲ It is fun to have a picnic when it is warm and sunny.

If it is cold, hot drinks and hot foods help to keep us warm.

▲ A bowl of hot soup is warming on a cold day.

Heaters

When it is cold we turn on heaters to help keep us warm indoors.

▲ A radiator warms the room because it is filled with hot water.

radiator

Sometimes we use a fire to heat a room. A fire may use electricity, gas, coal or wood to warm us.

▲ A fire makes us feel warm and cosy when it is cold outside.

Hot air rises

When we have heaters on in the house, they warm the air. The hot air rises to the top of the house.

▲ This special photograph shows the hottest parts of the house. They are the red and yellow parts.

A burner heats the air inside this balloon. The hot air is lighter and makes the balloon rise into the sky.

burner

What would happen if the burner was turned off?

Cooking

We use heat to cook food. A hot toaster or grill turns bread into toast.

slice of bread

Can you change the toast back into bread?

toast

Heat soon fries a raw egg.
You cannot fry an egg in a cold pan.

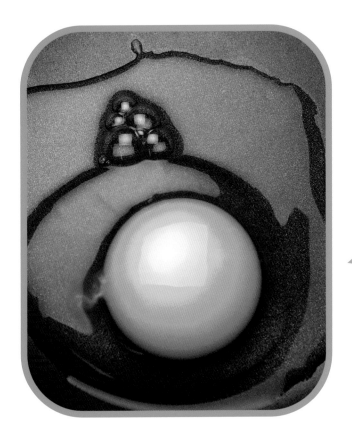

▼ Which egg would
you prefer
to eat?

raw egg

fried
egg

Melting

When this candle wax gets hot, it becomes runny. This is called melting. When it cools, the wax becomes hard again.

The wax at the top melts and runs down the candle.

melted wax

If you heat a bar of chocolate, it will become soft and runny.

Melted chocolate can be used as a dip for strawberries.

Freezing

If you cool water enough it will turn into ice. This is called freezing. A machine called a freezer turns water into ice.

An ice cube is frozen water. Ice cubes cool our drinks when it is hot. What happens to the ice after a while?

When the weather is very cold, water outside can freeze.

The water in this pond has become frozen so the ducks cannot swim.

Fresh food

If the weather is hot, our food will soon go bad. Food stays fresh for longer if we keep it cool.

We can use a fridge to keep our food fresh. It is very cold inside a fridge.

We freeze some food. When it is frozen, it will keep for a very long time.

▲ Frozen food is kept in a freezer. We have to thaw it before we can eat it.

Feathers and fur

Birds have feathers to keep them warm when it is cold.

This snowy owl has layers of feathers to keep it warm.

Some other animals have thick fur or long hair to keep them warm.

▲ A polar bear has thick white fur all over to keep it warm. It even has fur on the bottom of its feet.

Plants

Plants need lots of warmth from the sun to grow leaves and flowers.

Sunflowers grow big and tall when it is hot and sunny.

Many trees lose their leaves in the autumn when the days get colder. They grow new leaves next spring when the weather is warmer.

▲ In summer, when it is sunny and warm, this oak tree grows lots of green leaves.

Things to do

Cold days

Which of these things would you like to do on a cold day?

a

b

c

d

Breakfast time

Match the halves to find a slice of toast and a fried egg.

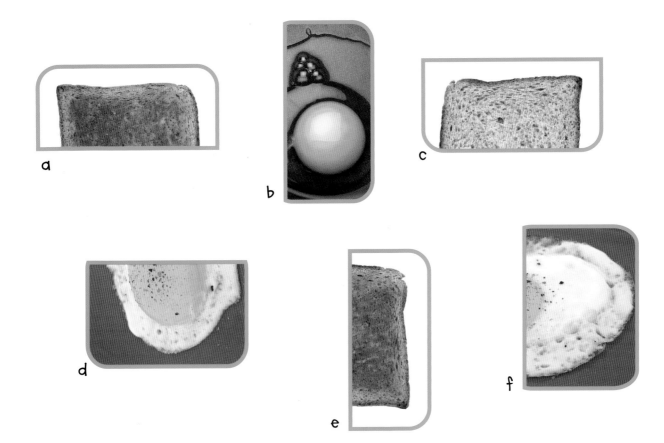

a

b

c

d

e

f

Talk back

What are your favourite hot foods?
What are your favourite cold foods?
What can you do to keep warm when it is cold?

Glossary

burner The part of a balloon that burns gas. The gas warms the air inside the balloon to make it fly.

picnic A meal usually eaten outdoors.

steam When water becomes very hot it makes steam.

thaw When something frozen warms up, or melts, so that it is no longer frozen.

Index